50 Stir it Up: The Art of Fusion Recipes

By: Kelly Johnson

Table of Contents

- Miso Tacos
- Tandoori Pizza
- Kimchi Quesadilla
- Curry Mac and Cheese
- Bulgogi Sliders
- Jerk Chicken Ramen
- Thai BBQ Wings
- Teriyaki Tostadas
- Coconut Alfredo Pasta
- Pho Burrito
- Shawarma Tacos
- Chimichurri Fried Rice
- Cajun Sushi Rolls
- Mole Pasta Bake
- Gochujang Grilled Cheese
- Pad Thai Burger
- Italian Banh Mi

- Wasabi Mashed Potatoes
- Greek Curry Bowl
- Udon Carbonara
- Plantain Gnocchi
- Samosa Empanadas
- Kalbi Tacos
- Jambalaya Risotto
- Bao Bun Sloppy Joes
- Moroccan Chili
- Sichuan Tacos
- Kimchi Carbonara
- Coconut Curry Lasagna
- Spicy Ramen Nachos
- Currywurst Hot Dogs
- Mediterranean Bibimbap
- Miso Glazed Meatloaf
- Cajun Tempura
- Thai Bolognese
- Sushi Nachos

- Chimichurri Ramen
- Teriyaki Meatballs
- Greek Quesadilla
- Indian Poutine
- Wasabi Guacamole Burgers
- Tikka Masala Shepherd's Pie
- Thai Enchiladas
- Tex-Mex Ramen
- Harissa Mac and Cheese
- Korean Corn Dogs
- Falafel Tacos
- Buffalo Tofu Bao
- Mango Salsa Pad Thai
- Spicy Tamarind Spaghetti

Miso Tacos

Ingredients

- 1 tbsp white miso paste
- 2 tbsp soy sauce
- 1 tbsp sesame oil
- 1 tbsp rice vinegar
- 1 tsp honey or maple syrup
- 1 block extra-firm tofu or protein of choice
- Corn tortillas
- Shredded cabbage
- Sliced radish
- Cilantro
- Lime wedges

Instructions

1. Press tofu to remove moisture, then cube.
2. Whisk miso, soy sauce, sesame oil, vinegar, and honey.
3. Marinate tofu for 30 mins, then pan-fry until golden.
4. Warm tortillas, layer with tofu, cabbage, radish, and cilantro.
5. Squeeze lime over the top before serving.

Tandoori Pizza

Ingredients

- 1 prepared pizza dough
- 1 cup cooked tandoori chicken (or cauliflower)
- 1/2 cup tomato sauce
- 1/4 cup Greek yogurt
- 1 tsp garam masala
- 1 cup mozzarella cheese
- Sliced red onion
- Cilantro

Instructions

1. Preheat oven to 475°F (245°C).
2. Mix tomato sauce with garam masala and spread on dough.
3. Add chicken, mozzarella, and onion.
4. Bake for 10–12 mins.
5. Drizzle with yogurt and sprinkle cilantro before serving.

Kimchi Quesadilla
Ingredients

- 2 large flour tortillas
- 1/2 cup chopped kimchi
- 1/2 cup shredded cheddar or mozzarella
- 1/4 cup sliced green onions
- 1 tsp sesame oil

Instructions

1. Heat sesame oil in pan, sauté kimchi for 3–5 mins.
2. Layer tortilla with cheese, kimchi, green onions, and top with another tortilla.
3. Grill until golden on both sides.
4. Slice and serve with sour cream or gochujang sauce.

Curry Mac and Cheese

Ingredients

- 8 oz elbow macaroni
- 2 tbsp butter
- 2 tbsp flour
- 2 cups milk
- 1 tbsp yellow curry powder
- 1 1/2 cups shredded sharp cheddar
- Salt to taste

Instructions

1. Cook pasta and drain.
2. In a saucepan, melt butter and whisk in flour for 1 min.
3. Add milk, curry powder, and whisk until thickened.
4. Stir in cheese until melted.
5. Combine sauce with pasta, season to taste.

Bulgogi Sliders

Ingredients

- 1/2 lb ground beef or thinly sliced ribeye
- 2 tbsp soy sauce
- 1 tbsp brown sugar
- 1 tsp sesame oil
- 2 garlic cloves, minced
- Slider buns
- Kimchi or slaw for topping
- Optional: mayo or sriracha

Instructions

1. Marinate beef in soy sauce, sugar, sesame oil, and garlic for 30 mins.
2. Cook in skillet until browned.
3. Toast buns, layer with beef, kimchi/slaw, and desired sauce.
4. Serve hot.

Jerk Chicken Ramen

Ingredients

- 1 pack ramen noodles
- 1 cup cooked jerk chicken, shredded
- 2 cups chicken broth
- 1/4 cup coconut milk
- 1 green onion, sliced
- Lime wedge

Instructions

1. Heat broth and coconut milk in pot.
2. Add noodles and cook per package.
3. Add jerk chicken to heat through.
4. Serve topped with green onions and a squeeze of lime.

Thai BBQ Wings
Ingredients

- 1 lb chicken wings
- 2 tbsp soy sauce
- 2 tbsp fish sauce
- 1 tbsp brown sugar
- 1 tbsp lime juice
- 1 tbsp garlic chili paste
- 1 tsp grated ginger

Instructions

1. Mix marinade ingredients and coat wings.
2. Marinate 1–2 hours.
3. Bake at 400°F (200°C) for 40 mins or grill until crispy.
4. Garnish with cilantro or crushed peanuts.

Teriyaki Tostadas

Ingredients

- 1 cup shredded chicken or tofu
- 1/4 cup teriyaki sauce
- Crispy tostada shells
- Shredded lettuce
- Diced pineapple
- Sliced green onion
- Sesame seeds

Instructions

1. Heat chicken with teriyaki sauce until coated and warm.
2. Layer tostada shells with lettuce, chicken, pineapple, and green onion.
3. Sprinkle sesame seeds and serve.

Coconut Alfredo Pasta

Ingredients

- 8 oz fettuccine
- 2 tbsp olive oil
- 3 garlic cloves, minced
- 1 can full-fat coconut milk
- 1/4 cup nutritional yeast or Parmesan
- Salt and pepper
- Fresh basil (optional)

Instructions

1. Cook pasta and reserve 1/4 cup water.
2. Sauté garlic in olive oil until fragrant.
3. Add coconut milk and bring to simmer.
4. Stir in cheese/nutritional yeast and pasta water.
5. Toss in pasta, season, and garnish with basil.

Pho Burrito

Ingredients

- 1 large flour tortilla
- 1/2 cup cooked rice noodles
- 1/2 cup shredded beef (or tofu)
- 1/4 cup pho broth (reduced until thick)
- Fresh basil, cilantro, and mint
- Sliced red onion
- Bean sprouts
- Hoisin and sriracha

Instructions

1. Warm tortilla and layer noodles, beef, herbs, onion, sprouts.
2. Drizzle thickened broth, hoisin, and sriracha.
3. Wrap burrito-style, then sear in a hot pan for 1–2 mins each side.
4. Slice and serve hot with a side of broth for dipping.

Shawarma Tacos

Ingredients

- 1/2 lb chicken thighs or chickpeas
- 1 tbsp shawarma spice blend
- 1 tbsp olive oil
- Small pita or flour tortillas
- Garlic yogurt sauce
- Pickled onions
- Chopped tomatoes and lettuce

Instructions

1. Season and cook chicken in olive oil until crispy.
2. Warm tortillas or pita, spread yogurt sauce.
3. Add meat, pickled onions, tomato, and lettuce.
4. Serve warm with extra garlic sauce on the side.

Chimichurri Fried Rice

Ingredients

- 2 cups day-old rice
- 1/2 cup chopped protein (steak, shrimp, tofu)
- 2 eggs
- 2 tbsp chimichurri sauce
- 1/4 cup chopped bell peppers
- 2 green onions, sliced
- Oil for frying

Instructions

1. Scramble eggs, set aside.
2. Cook protein until done, then add peppers and rice.
3. Stir-fry for 3–5 mins, add eggs back in.
4. Stir in chimichurri and green onions just before serving.

Cajun Sushi Rolls

Ingredients

- 1 cup sushi rice
- 1 tbsp rice vinegar
- 1/2 cup blackened shrimp or chicken
- Thin avocado slices
- Cajun mayo (mayo + Cajun seasoning)
- Nori sheets

Instructions

1. Cook rice, mix with vinegar.
2. Place rice on nori, add shrimp, avocado, and drizzle Cajun mayo.
3. Roll tightly and slice.
4. Serve with soy sauce and extra spicy mayo.

Mole Pasta Bake

Ingredients

- 8 oz penne or rigatoni
- 1 cup mole sauce (homemade or store-bought)
- 1/2 cup shredded chicken
- 1/2 cup Monterey Jack cheese
- 1/4 cup cotija cheese
- Chopped cilantro

Instructions

1. Cook pasta and mix with mole and chicken.
2. Transfer to baking dish, top with cheeses.
3. Bake at 375°F (190°C) for 20–25 mins.
4. Garnish with cilantro and serve hot.

Gochujang Grilled Cheese

Ingredients

- 2 slices sourdough or thick bread
- 1 tbsp butter
- 1 tsp gochujang
- 2 slices cheddar or mozzarella
- Kimchi (optional)

Instructions

1. Mix butter and gochujang, spread on outer bread sides.
2. Layer cheese and kimchi inside.
3. Grill in skillet until golden and melty.
4. Serve with extra gochujang or honey drizzle.

Pad Thai Burger

Ingredients

- 1 ground chicken or plant-based patty
- 1 tbsp peanut sauce
- Shredded carrots
- Chopped peanuts
- Cilantro
- Pickled onions
- Brioche bun

Instructions

1. Grill or pan-cook patty.
2. Toast bun, spread peanut sauce.
3. Top patty with carrots, peanuts, cilantro, and pickled onions.
4. Assemble and enjoy that sweet-salty-crunchy fusion.

Italian Banh Mi

Ingredients

- 1 small baguette
- 1/4 cup sliced prosciutto or salami
- Fresh mozzarella slices
- Pickled carrots and daikon
- Basil and arugula
- Balsamic glaze

Instructions

1. Slice and toast baguette lightly.
2. Layer meat, cheese, pickled veggies, herbs.
3. Drizzle with balsamic glaze.
4. Press gently and serve sandwich-style.

Wasabi Mashed Potatoes

Ingredients

- 1.5 lbs Yukon Gold potatoes
- 2 tbsp butter
- 1/4 cup milk or cream
- 1–2 tsp wasabi paste (to taste)
- Salt to taste
- Chopped scallions (optional)

Instructions

1. Boil potatoes until tender, mash with butter and milk.
2. Stir in wasabi and salt.
3. Mix until creamy and smooth.
4. Garnish with scallions or sesame seeds.

Greek Curry Bowl

Ingredients

- 1/2 cup cooked quinoa or rice
- 1/2 cup chickpeas
- 1/4 cup tzatziki
- 1/2 cup roasted curry-spiced veggies (zucchini, peppers, onion)
- Kalamata olives
- Feta cheese

Instructions

1. Roast veggies tossed with olive oil and curry powder at 400°F for 25 mins.
2. Layer base with quinoa, then chickpeas, roasted veg.
3. Top with tzatziki, feta, and olives.
4. Serve warm or cold.

Udon Carbonara

Ingredients

- 1 pack udon noodles
- 2 eggs
- 1/4 cup grated Parmesan
- 1/4 cup cooked bacon or mushrooms
- 1 garlic clove, minced
- Black pepper

Instructions

1. Cook udon and drain, reserving a bit of water.
2. Sauté garlic and bacon/mushrooms.
3. Whisk eggs with Parmesan.
4. Toss noodles with garlic mix, remove from heat, then add egg mixture, stirring quickly to create a creamy sauce.
5. Finish with cracked pepper.

Plantain Gnocchi

Ingredients

- 2 ripe plantains (yellow with black spots)
- 1/2 cup flour (plus more for dusting)
- 1 egg yolk
- Salt to taste
- Butter, garlic, and sage for sauce

Instructions

1. Boil peeled plantains until tender, mash until smooth.
2. Mix with flour, egg yolk, and salt to form a dough.
3. Roll into ropes, cut into gnocchi pieces, and gently shape.
4. Boil until they float (about 2 mins), then sauté in butter with garlic and sage until golden.

Samosa Empanadas

Ingredients

- 1 cup mashed potatoes
- 1/2 cup peas
- 1/2 tsp garam masala
- 1/4 tsp cumin
- 1/4 tsp turmeric
- Empanada dough rounds
- Oil for brushing or frying

Instructions

1. Mix potatoes, peas, and spices.
2. Spoon filling into dough, fold and seal with fork.
3. Bake at 400°F (200°C) for 15–20 mins or fry until golden.
4. Serve with chutney or yogurt sauce.

Kalbi Tacos

Ingredients

- 1/2 lb thin-sliced short rib or bulgogi beef
- Kalbi marinade (soy sauce, garlic, sugar, sesame oil)
- Corn tortillas
- Kimchi or cabbage slaw
- Green onions
- Sriracha mayo

Instructions

1. Marinate meat 1–2 hours, grill or pan-sear until caramelized.
2. Warm tortillas, add beef, slaw, green onion, and drizzle with sriracha mayo.
3. Serve hot.

Jambalaya Risotto

Ingredients

- 1 cup Arborio rice
- 1/2 onion, diced
- 1/2 bell pepper, diced
- 1/2 lb sausage or shrimp
- 3 cups chicken stock (warm)
- 1 tsp Cajun seasoning
- Butter and Parmesan (optional)

Instructions

1. Sauté onion and pepper, add sausage/shrimp and cook through.
2. Stir in rice and toast for 2 mins.
3. Gradually add stock, stirring until absorbed.
4. Add Cajun seasoning and finish with butter/cheese if desired.

Bao Bun Sloppy Joes

Ingredients

- 1/2 lb ground beef or tofu
- 2 tbsp hoisin sauce
- 1 tbsp soy sauce
- 1 tsp garlic and ginger
- Steamed bao buns
- Pickled carrots and cucumbers

Instructions

1. Brown beef/tofu, add sauces and aromatics.
2. Simmer until thick.
3. Fill bao with mixture, add pickled veggies.
4. Serve with sesame seeds or cilantro.

Moroccan Chili

Ingredients

- 1/2 lb ground lamb or lentils
- 1 can diced tomatoes
- 1 can chickpeas
- 1/2 onion, diced
- 1 tsp cinnamon
- 1 tsp cumin
- 1/2 tsp paprika
- Harissa or chili paste (optional heat)

Instructions

1. Sauté onion and meat/lentils.
2. Add spices, tomatoes, and chickpeas.
3. Simmer 20–30 mins.
4. Serve with couscous or flatbread.

Sichuan Tacos

Ingredients

- 1/2 lb ground pork or tofu
- 1 tbsp doubanjiang (chili bean paste)
- 1 tbsp soy sauce
- 1 tsp Sichuan peppercorns (crushed)
- Corn tortillas
- Shredded cucumber or pickled veg

Instructions

1. Cook pork/tofu with chili paste, soy sauce, and peppercorns.
2. Toast tortillas, fill with spicy mix.
3. Top with fresh veggies for cool contrast.

Kimchi Carbonara

Ingredients

- 8 oz spaghetti
- 2 eggs
- 1/2 cup chopped kimchi
- 1/4 cup Parmesan
- 2 tbsp bacon or mushroom
- Black pepper

Instructions

1. Cook pasta, reserve some water.
2. Sauté bacon/mushrooms and kimchi.
3. Whisk eggs and cheese.
4. Toss pasta with kimchi, then remove from heat and add egg mix quickly.
5. Stir to coat and serve with extra pepper.

Coconut Curry Lasagna
Ingredients

- 9 lasagna noodles
- 2 cups coconut curry sauce (yellow or red)
- 1 cup cooked veggies (zucchini, carrots, spinach)
- 1/2 cup shredded mozzarella
- Fresh basil

Instructions

1. Boil noodles, layer sauce, veggies, cheese, repeat.
2. Bake at 375°F (190°C) for 30–35 mins.
3. Top with basil and a drizzle of coconut milk.

Spicy Ramen Nachos

Ingredients

- 1 pack ramen noodles (uncooked)
- 1/2 cup shredded cheese
- 1/2 cup cooked ground meat or tofu
- Sriracha or gochujang
- Green onions
- Sesame seeds

Instructions

1. Break uncooked ramen into chunks and lightly toast in oven or pan.
2. Top with cheese and meat, broil until melty.
3. Drizzle with sriracha, add onions and sesame seeds.
4. Eat with fingers or chopsticks—your call.

Currywurst Hot Dogs

Ingredients

- 4 bratwursts or hot dogs
- 1/2 cup ketchup
- 1 tbsp curry powder
- 1 tsp smoked paprika
- 1 tbsp vinegar
- Soft buns
- Chopped onions or fries (optional topping)

Instructions

1. Grill or pan-fry sausages.
2. Simmer ketchup, curry powder, paprika, and vinegar until thick.
3. Spoon sauce over dogs in buns.
4. Top with onions or fries if you're feeling wild.

Mediterranean Bibimbap

Ingredients

- Cooked rice or quinoa
- Roasted eggplant, zucchini, and cherry tomatoes
- Kalamata olives and crumbled feta
- Fried egg
- Tzatziki or lemon tahini sauce

Instructions

1. Arrange veggies and toppings over warm rice.
2. Add a sunny-side-up egg.
3. Drizzle with sauce and mix before eating.

Miso Glazed Meatloaf

Ingredients

- 1 lb ground beef or turkey
- 1/4 cup breadcrumbs
- 1 egg
- 1 tbsp miso paste
- 1 tbsp soy sauce
- 1 tbsp honey
- 1 tsp garlic

Instructions

1. Mix meat, egg, breadcrumbs, and garlic. Shape into loaf.
2. Bake at 375°F (190°C) for 30 mins.
3. Mix miso, soy, and honey, then glaze meatloaf and bake 10 more mins.
4. Slice and serve with rice or greens.

Cajun Tempura

Ingredients

- Shrimp or veggies (zucchini, mushrooms, bell peppers)
- 1/2 cup flour + 1/2 cup cornstarch
- 1 egg
- 1/2 cup cold seltzer water
- 1 tsp Cajun seasoning
- Oil for frying

Instructions

1. Mix flour, cornstarch, egg, seltzer, and seasoning.
2. Dip ingredients in batter and fry until golden.
3. Serve with spicy remoulade or aioli.

Thai Bolognese

Ingredients

- 1/2 lb ground pork or beef
- 1 tbsp red curry paste
- 1/2 cup coconut milk
- 1 tbsp fish sauce
- 1 tsp sugar
- Cooked spaghetti or rice noodles

Instructions

1. Cook meat, add curry paste and coconut milk.
2. Stir in fish sauce and sugar, simmer until thick.
3. Toss with noodles and top with Thai basil or lime zest.

Sushi Nachos

Ingredients

- Wonton chips or crispy rice squares
- Diced raw or cooked fish (tuna, salmon, shrimp)
- Avocado, cucumber, jalapeño
- Sriracha mayo and unagi sauce
- Sesame seeds and green onions

Instructions

1. Layer chips with fish, avocado, and cucumber.
2. Drizzle sauces, sprinkle toppings.
3. Eat immediately for max crunch.

Chimichurri Ramen

Ingredients

- Instant ramen (no seasoning packet)
- 1/4 cup fresh chimichurri sauce
- Sliced steak, grilled veggies, or tofu
- Soft-boiled egg (optional)

Instructions

1. Cook ramen noodles and drain.
2. Toss in chimichurri and top with your protein/veg of choice.
3. Add egg if desired, and serve with chili flakes.

Teriyaki Meatballs

Ingredients

- 1 lb ground chicken or beef
- 1/4 cup breadcrumbs
- 1 egg
- 1/2 tsp garlic and ginger
- 1/4 cup teriyaki sauce

Instructions

1. Mix meat, egg, crumbs, and seasoning. Shape into balls.
2. Bake at 400°F (200°C) for 15–20 mins.
3. Toss in warmed teriyaki sauce before serving.
4. Serve with rice or in lettuce cups.

Greek Quesadilla
Ingredients

- Flour tortillas
- Crumbled feta and shredded mozzarella
- Spinach and sun-dried tomatoes
- Kalamata olives (chopped)
- Tzatziki for dipping

Instructions

1. Fill tortilla with cheese, veggies, and olives.
2. Grill until golden and melty.
3. Cut and serve with tzatziki.

Indian Poutine

Ingredients

- Crispy fries or potato wedges
- Paneer or cheese curds
- Masala gravy (onion, tomato, garam masala, cream)
- Cilantro garnish

Instructions

1. Make a simple masala gravy and keep warm.
2. Top hot fries with cheese and ladle on the sauce.
3. Sprinkle with chopped cilantro and dig in.

Wasabi Guacamole Burgers

Ingredients

- 1 lb ground beef or plant-based patties
- 2 avocados
- 1 tsp wasabi paste (adjust to taste)
- Juice of 1 lime
- Brioche buns
- Lettuce, tomato, red onion

Instructions

1. Mash avocado, mix in wasabi and lime juice for guac.
2. Grill or pan-fry burger patties.
3. Toast buns and assemble with lettuce, patty, wasabi guac, and toppings.

Tikka Masala Shepherd's Pie

Ingredients

- 1/2 lb ground lamb or lentils
- 1/2 onion, diced
- 1/2 cup tikka masala sauce
- 2 cups mashed potatoes
- Butter and cilantro (optional)

Instructions

1. Brown lamb with onion, stir in tikka sauce.
2. Pour into a baking dish and spread mashed potatoes on top.
3. Bake at 375°F (190°C) for 20–25 mins.
4. Broil for a golden top and garnish with cilantro.

Thai Enchiladas

Ingredients

- 1 cup shredded chicken or tofu
- 1/2 cup Thai peanut sauce
- 4 tortillas
- Shredded cheese (mozzarella or jack)
- Lime wedges and chopped peanuts

Instructions

1. Mix filling with peanut sauce.
2. Roll into tortillas and place in a baking dish.
3. Top with cheese and bake at 375°F (190°C) for 20 mins.
4. Garnish with lime and peanuts.

Tex-Mex Ramen

Ingredients

- 1 pack ramen noodles
- 1/2 cup ground beef or black beans
- Taco seasoning
- 1/4 cup corn and diced tomatoes
- Shredded cheddar and jalapeños

Instructions

1. Cook beef/beans with taco seasoning.
2. Cook ramen, drain, and mix with seasoned filling.
3. Top with cheddar, corn mix, and jalapeños.

Harissa Mac and Cheese

Ingredients

- 8 oz macaroni
- 2 tbsp butter
- 2 tbsp flour
- 2 cups milk
- 1 1/2 cups shredded cheese
- 1–2 tbsp harissa paste

Instructions

1. Make roux with butter and flour, whisk in milk until thick.
2. Stir in cheese and harissa.
3. Toss with cooked pasta.
4. Bake for extra texture or eat as is.

Korean Corn Dogs

Ingredients

- Hot dogs or mozzarella sticks
- Skewer sticks
- 1 cup flour, 1 egg, 1/2 cup milk
- 1 cup panko
- Sugar (for dusting)
- Oil for frying

Instructions

1. Skewer and chill hot dogs/cheese.
2. Dip in thick batter, roll in panko.
3. Deep-fry until golden.
4. Dust lightly with sugar and drizzle with ketchup or mustard.

Falafel Tacos

Ingredients

- Falafel (homemade or frozen)
- Pita or corn tortillas
- Hummus or tahini
- Shredded lettuce, cucumber, tomato
- Pickled onions

Instructions

1. Warm falafel and tortillas.
2. Spread hummus, add falafel and veggies.
3. Top with pickled onions and a drizzle of lemon tahini.

Buffalo Tofu Bao
Ingredients

- Steamed bao buns
- Crispy tofu cubes
- Buffalo sauce
- Cabbage slaw
- Vegan ranch or blue cheese drizzle

Instructions

1. Toss crispy tofu in buffalo sauce.
2. Fill bao with slaw, tofu, and drizzle.
3. Serve warm with extra sauce on the side.

Mango Salsa Pad Thai

Ingredients

- Rice noodles
- 1/2 cup diced mango
- 1/4 cup red onion and red pepper
- 1 egg (optional)
- Pad Thai sauce (tamarind, fish sauce, sugar, lime)
- Crushed peanuts and cilantro

Instructions

1. Sauté onion, pepper, and scrambled egg.
2. Add noodles and sauce, cook through.
3. Toss in mango, top with peanuts and herbs.

Spicy Tamarind Spaghetti

Ingredients

- 8 oz spaghetti
- 2 tbsp tamarind paste
- 1 tbsp chili crisp or sambal
- 1 tbsp soy sauce
- 2 cloves garlic, minced
- Green onions and sesame seeds

Instructions

1. Cook spaghetti, reserve some water.
2. Sauté garlic, stir in tamarind, chili, and soy.
3. Toss noodles with sauce, add water if needed.
4. Garnish and serve hot.